On the Edge SKATEBOARDING

Patty Segovia

Designed by
Matthew Eberhart, Evil Eye Design, Inc.

Contributing consultant
Arlie John Carstens

Manufactured and printed in the United States.

Meredith BOOKS

First Edition
ISBN 978-0-696-23540-5
We welcome your comments and suggestions.
Write to us at: Meredith Books,
1716 Locust St., Des Moines, IA 50309-3023
Visit us at meredithbooks.com

Photo Credits:
(c) Patty Segovia, pages 1 (right), 2, 3, 4 (top right, bottom), 5 (middle right, bottom left), 6, 8 (top left, middle left, bottom left, bottom right), 9 (top left, bottom left), 11–18, 20, 21 (top, middle right), 22–24; (c) Jody Morris, cover, pages 1 (left), 7; (c) Brendan Klein, page 19; (c) etnies Girl, page 10; Shutterstock.com: (c) Reha Mark, page 4 (top left); (c) Vladimir Ivanovich Danilov, page 4 (middle); (c) Galina Barskaya, pages 5 (top), 9 (right); (c) Jaimie Duplass, page 5 (bottom); (c) Tihis, pages 8 (top right), 21 (bottom left); (c) Afaizal, page 21 (bottom right)

Cara-Beth Burnside

HOMETOWN:
Encinitas, California

BIRTHDAY:
July 23

FAVORITE TYPE OF RIDING:
Pools and vert

STANCE:
Goofy

Q&A with Cara-Beth Burnside

How old were you when you started?
11

What got you into the sport?
A new skatepark opened down the street.

Any advice for beginners?
Just stick around positive people who encourage your passion.

What type of music do you listen to?
All kinds. Just depends on what I'm doing. While I skate, I like to listen to metal or reggae music.

Favorite groups?
Steel Pulse, Dido, Scorpions, Led Zeppelin, Ozzy Osbourne

Highlights of your career?
1998 Olympics at Nagano, Japan: Snowboarding fourth place; first pro-model signature shoe with Vans; first place All Girl Skate Jam; cover of *Thrasher* magazine

Signature move/favorite skate trick?
Hand plant/feeble to fakie, judo airs

Signature move/favorite snowboarding trick?
My favorite snowboarding trick is the McTwist, because it's fun to do.

How did you get to be you?
Lots of hard work and determination

What do you like to do outside of snowboarding/skateboarding?
Eat organic foods and cook healthy meals, surf, stretch, read, hang out with my friends, work on my grip tape company

Backside Air on Vert

To do this trick you must know how to drop into a vert ramp and maintain enough speed to make it to the top of the opposing wall. But don't worry, a backside air is one of the most basic halfpipe tricks you can do. It is also some of the most fun you will have in your life!

1. Drop into the ramp with enough speed to make it to the top of the opposing wall. When crossing the flat bottom of the ramp, begin compressing your knees as you approach the oncoming transition (aka opposing wall).
2. Once you get to the top of the wall, your front wheels will hit the coping (steel pipe) at the edge of the ramp. As this happens, you must spring upward into the air. This motion will shoot you up above the deck of the ramp and your body will naturally travel through the air. At this point, the ramp will be directly beneath you.
3. Remember: Don't leap away from the ramp as you spring off the coping; doing that will cause you to fly out onto the flat bottom of the ramp. Ouch!
4. Once in the air, use your front hand to grab the heelside of the board, between your heels. Make sure to grab the board nearer to your front leg, not between your legs.
5. As you gain air, you will travel in the direction your toes are facing while turning backside. Square your shoulders and start to compress your knees again for landing.
6. As you turn 180 degrees, look down to spot your landing in the transition. Land smoothly with all four wheels at the same time; doing this will help you keep speed through the flat bottom as you set up for an air on the next wall.

General Tips

These skating tips will help you become an awesome skateboarder, safely! Skateboarding can be a dangerous activity, but injuries can be minimized when proper equipment is used and protective gear is worn. Whether you're skating streets, ramps, or skate parks, always remember to wear a helmet and pads to help reduce the risk of injury.

make sure you have quality equipment: It is important to have a well-built skateboard, not an inexpensive version from a toy store. This will minimize product defects that could cause the board to break down during normal use. Your pads and helmet should be top quality, and protective equipment should fit properly.

never skate near traffic: Never skate on busy streets or in places with a lot of pedestrian and bicycle traffic! Colliding with a walker, bicyclist, or automobile can leave you severely injured.

how good are you? Know your skill level so that you won't try tricks that are too advanced. Always work your way up from easiest to more difficult tricks. Like other achievements in life, skateboarding requires dedication and time.

fast friends: Bring a buddy whenever you go skating, but limit one person per skateboard. It's good to have a friend around in case anything goes wrong.

know how to fall: Knowing how to fall properly can reduce your chance of injury. Learn to fall by practicing on the grass or other soft surface. When you begin to lose your balance, crouch down, reducing the distance of the fall. If you find yourself falling, tuck, roll, and try not to catch yourself with your hands or arms. Teach yourself to not put your hands in front of you during a fall—this could lead to a break or bad muscle sprain. If at all possible, relax your body when falling rather than falling stiff.

stretch: Don't forget to stretch and warm up before you skate; you don't want to pull any muscles.

water: Skateboarding is a vigorous athletic activity; always remember to drink plenty of water before, during, and after skateboarding. Dehydration can cause muscle cramps, nausea, and a feeling of lightheadedness.

Kevin Staab

HOMETOWN:
Encinitas, California

BIRTHDAY:
April 22

FAVORITE TYPE OF RIDING:
All skateboarding, but pools and ramps are the best

STANCE:
Regular

Q&A with Kevin Staab

How old were you when you started?
8

What were you doing by the age of 10?
Skating

What got you into the sport?
When I was younger, I kept getting skateboards for Christmas and my birthday, so I felt it was a sign that I should skate.

What advice would you give a kid about skateboarding?
Set goals for yourself.

Any advice for beginners?
Have fun with skateboarding.

Highlights of your career?
We recently finished the Tony Hawk Secret Skatepark Tour, which was unannounced. We randomly went to eight different skateparks with a two- to three-hour notice. The Montana stop was the only one that was announced, because it was the grand opening of a skatepark. There were 8,000 people there. We also did separate tours at Six Flags Magic Mountain parks called Tony Hawk Grand Jam that included BMXers, skaters, and motorcycle riders. It was super fun.

Signature move/favorite trick?
Backside ollies and frontside grinds

How did you get to be you?
I always saw a hippie-surfer dude named Ted (who lived down the street from my house) skating.

How does a kid get to be as good as you?
It is important to set goals. As a kid, I used to have a list of tricks I wanted to learn. I would tape a piece of paper to the bottom of my skateboard with a list of tricks I was working on at the time. I was very goal-driven.

What do you like to do outside of skateboarding?
Hang out with my family and friends

Goals for the future?
To always remain around skateboarding and remain an influence in vert skateboarding

Frontside Lien Air on Vert

A lien air is simply a variation of a frontside air—one of the most basic, essential tricks in vert skating. This trick has style!

1. Drop into the ramp with enough speed to make it to the top of the opposing wall. When crossing the flat bottom of the ramp, compress your knees as you approach the oncoming transition.
2. As your front wheels pop off the coping, you must spring upward into the air while traveling with your chest facing the deck of the ramp. This is what makes it a frontside air.
3. Once in the air, grab the nose, or front heelside edge, of the board with your leading hand. Remember: Don't leap away from the ramp as you spring off the coping.
4. As you're in the air, look over your front shoulder to spot the transition below. As you complete the 180-degree arc of your air, square your shoulders and compress your knees again for landing.
5. Land smoothly with all four wheels at the same time; maintain your speed through the flat bottom as you set up for an air on the next wall.

PRO
ROOK
DO • ESCONDIDO • ESCONDIDO •

Safety Gear

WEAR YOUR PROTECTIVE EQUIPMENT

Wearing your helmet, wrist guards, and knee and elbow pads will truly reduce the chance of fractures and sprains and everything else that goes along with getting hurt.

helmet: A helmet is a must for all skateboarders. Made out of a high-density, impact-resistant ABS plastic outer shell and a shock absorbing, thick inner liner, helmets can protect you from head injuries. Make sure to get a skate-specific helmet.

knee pads: Knee pads protect with hard outer shells and foam padding. Knee pads are an excellent safety precaution for both street and ramp skaters. Ramp skaters automatically fall to their knees when they fall, so knee pads are mandatory.

elbow pads: Elbow pads have molded caps with lightweight pads for protection.

wrist guards: Wrist guards protect your wrists and palms. A good thing about wrist guards is they take the impact in a fall instead of your hands.

skateboarding-specific shoes: Skateboarding-specific shoes have extra-durable material at the foot's ollie points and cushiony soles to help minimize heel bruise and better absorb the impact of landing tricks.

Lauren Perkins

HOMETOWN:
Huntington Beach, California

BIRTHDAY:
December 27

FAVORITE TYPE OF RIDING:
Street skating

STANCE:
Goofy

Q&A with Lauren Perkins

How old were you when you started?
I was about 6 years old when I got my first skateboard.

What were you doing by the age of 10?
School and skateboarding

What got you into the sport?
My dad had a skateboard lying around the house when I was super little, and I would try to ride it. Then as I got a little bit older, they put a skatepark in by my house, and so for my sixth birthday, my mom and dad got me my first skateboard.

Any advice for beginners?
Don't give up. It might seem hard at first, but just keep at it!

What type of music do you listen to?
A little bit of everything

Favorite groups?
Too many favorites to have just one

Highlights of your career?
Silver medal in the 2006 X Games; bronze medal in 2004 X Games; and silver medal in the 2004 Gravity Games

Signature move/favorite trick?
A kickflip, because it's pretty simple and looks really good

How did you get to be you?
Just doing the things in life that make me happy and surrounding myself with good people

How does a kid get to be as good as you?
Just keep practicing and never give up.

What do you like to do outside of skateboarding?
Outside of skateboarding, I love to hang out with my friends and do stuff with them. I also enjoy motorcycle riding with my dad.

Ollie to Frontside 5-0 Grind on Ledge

This is a combination of two tricks. To do it, you should first know how to ollie up onto a ledge and how to do a basic grind on your rear truck axle.

1. Approach the ledge with enough speed to ollie up onto it. To do this, do not skate directly at the ledge. Instead, skate up next to the ledge at an angle, riding in the direction you're going to ollie. To do a frontside 5-0, your chest must face the ledge as you skate up to it. (To do a backside 5-0, you would begin the trick with your backside to the ledge.)
2. Ollie with enough pop to get your whole body and skateboard well above the lip of the ledge.
3. As you come down, you want only the axle of your rear truck to make contact with the ledge. Do not grind both trucks on the ledge. (That's a different trick, called a 50/50 axle grind.)
4. Once your rear truck has made contact, you will begin grinding the ledge; this will feel awesome!
5. Keep most of your weight on your back foot and use your front leg to steer the trick.
6. Once you've ground the ledge as far as you'd like to go, pop another ollie back onto the ground and ride away smoothly.

Skateboard Components

A skateboard has five main parts: deck, wheels, trucks, grip tape, and bearings.

deck: Skateboards normally have a width between 7 and 8 1/2 inches and a length of 29 to 34 inches. Decks are made from thin layers of maple wood. The layers are pressed together with glue. Days later, after the wood cures, the final shape is cut, the edges are sanded, and the graphics are silk-screened. The curvature of a skateboard deck is called concave. The shape of the deck is sort of "scooped" like a spoon and this makes the board stronger.

wheels: Quality wheels are made of a urethane formula, which is a hard rubber substance that performs well on different surfaces. Every wheel is special; you may want to try out different hardnesses and sizes as you improve. The two classifications for skateboard wheels are durometer and size. The higher the durometer, the harder the wheel. Soft wheels give a smoother ride that is ideal for cruising, while street skating requires harder wheels. In the pool or ramp, you may want to start with a softer, more gripping wheel but later change to a harder wheel.

The size of the wheel is measured in millimeters and can range from 52 mm to 78 mm. Smaller boards have smaller wheels, while larger boards have bigger, wider wheels. Large, soft wheels, like the ones you may see on a longboard, generally go faster and have more grip. Smaller, harder wheels are lightweight, which makes it easier to perform tricks.

trucks: The trucks hold the wheels onto the board and allow the wheels to turn. The parts of a truck are the base plate, kingpin, axle, hanger, and bushing. The base plate is bolted to the bottom of the board. The kingpin is the large bolt that connects the hanger to the base plate. You can adjust the kingpin to make your trucks looser or tighter.

grip tape: All decks are covered with a sticky-backed sandpaper surface called grip tape. It is applied to the top of the deck so that your feet grip while riding.

bearings: Bearings sit between the wheel and the axle and allow the wheels to spin. There are two bearings per skate wheel. The nuts and bolts hold the board together. Skateboard bolts are made out of high-grade steel.

Kris Markovich

HOMETOWN: Carlsbad, California
BIRTHDAY: October 9
FAVORITE TYPE OF RIDING: Street and random concrete
STANCE: Regular

Q&A with Kris Markovich

How old were you when you started?
13

What got you into the sport?
All my friends surfed, and I wasn't allowed to go to the beach without my parents, so I skated instead.

What were you doing before you started skateboarding?
Playing baseball and football

Any advice for beginners?
Learn how to ride your skateboard before you try to learn every trick in the book. It makes learning tricks easier down the line. It's better to be able to do fewer tricks right than more tricks wrong!

What type of music do you listen to?
Rock 'n' roll

Favorite groups?
Hellacopters, Turbonegro, Black Sabbath

Signature move/favorite trick?
I don't really have a signature move. I'm just kind of known for skating fast. Everything feels better when it's done faster.

How did you get to be you?
This sounds lame, but I had a really good family life growing up and I just kind of listened to my parents, and they helped me out a lot.

How does a kid get to be as good as you?
Skate as much as you can on everything you can! The more terrain you can skate, the better you will be. Even if you're a street skater, try and skate vert or pools or anything you can. Believe me, it will help you in the end. There is nothing worse than seeing a really good street skater flailing around on some tranny (transitional materials, such as the cement in skateparks).

What do you like to do outside of skateboarding?
I'm an artist as well as a skateboarder, so I spend most of my time when I'm not skating in my studio, painting. I like to read a lot and play the guitar.

Fakie Big Spin over Gap

This is a fun trick you can do over obstacles and on mini ramps. The board spins 360 degrees, while the skateboarder does a body varial in the same direction, which is simply rotating 180 degrees in the air. Before attempting this trick you should comfortably know how to do a big ollie over a gap, a 360 shuvit, and a body varial.

1. Start off rolling backwards (fakie) with enough speed to pop an ollie over the gap.
2. As you approach the gap, wind your body in the opposite direction you intend to spin and get ready to ollie. The extra spring created by your wind-up will provide momentum needed to clear the gap while performing the 360 shuvit.
3. Spring off the tail of the board and begin the first 270 degrees of the shuvit, while at the same time rotating your body the first 90 degrees. This is easier than you think.
4. Don't let the board get away from you, keep your body traveling over it as much as possible.
5. At this point, try to catch the board in midair with your feet and rotate the remaining 90 degrees with the board.
6. Land with both feet firmly on the deck and all four wheels touching down at the same time. Ride away smoothly.

VISA
THRASHER
Velvet
KRONIK ENERGY
SCUM
POWELL
gro
SKATEXXA

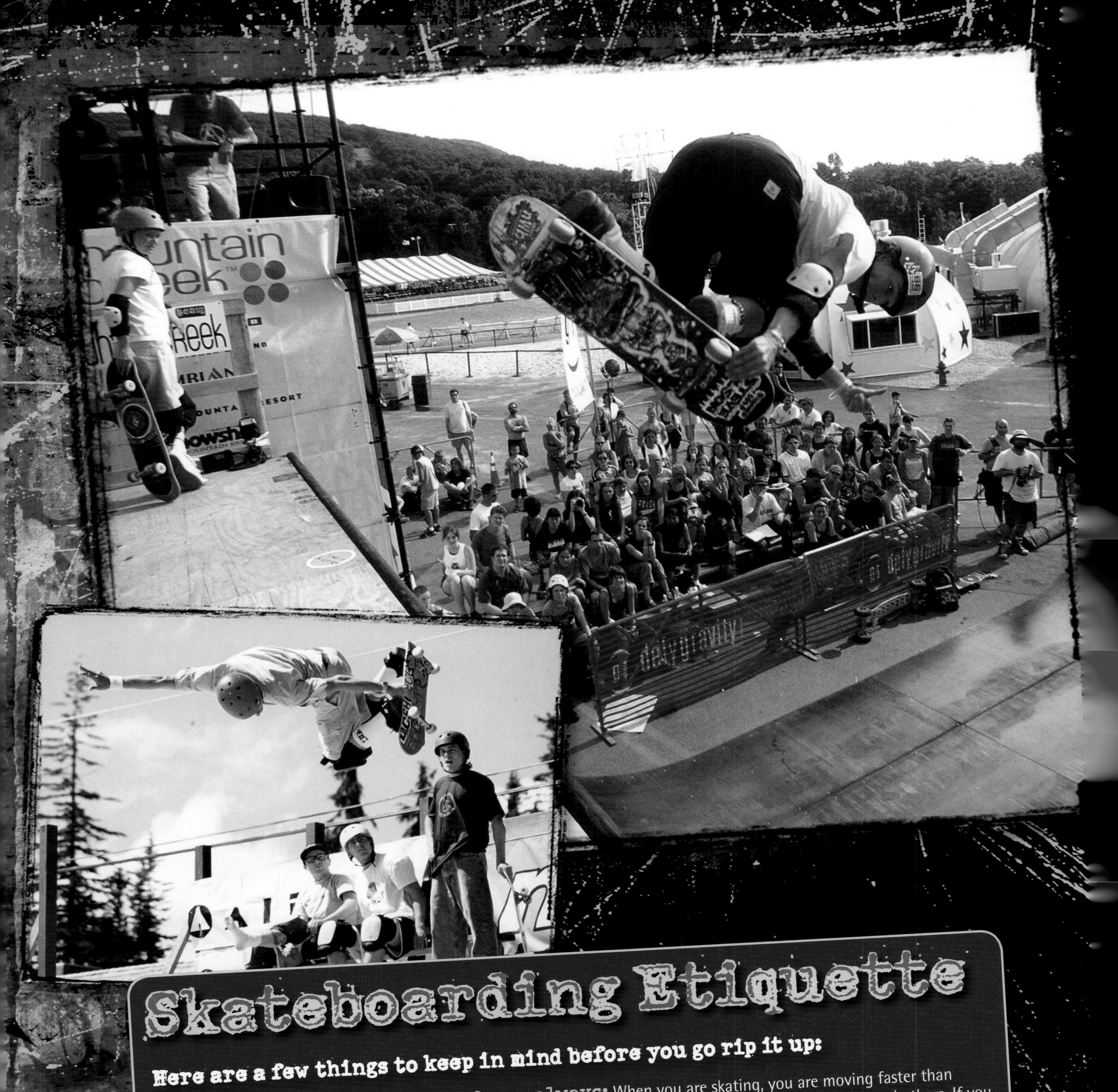

Skateboarding Etiquette

Here are a few things to keep in mind before you go rip it up:

- **pedestrians have the right of way, always:** When you are skating, you are moving faster than someone who is walking. It is your job to avoid him/her, not the other way around. Be thoughtful around others. If you come up behind a person, stay alert as he/she may unknowingly move in front of you at the last minute. Pass slowly. If you do collide with a person, apologize and make sure no one is hurt.
- **skate area:** When learning to skate or practicing new tricks, make sure to practice in an area that is not crowded.
- **one run, then wait your turn:** You must wait until the person on the ramp or bowl has completed his/her run, either by kicking out or bailing. Once that person clears the skate area it will be your turn to go—if someone else doesn't drop in before you.

Heidi Fitzgerald

HOMETOWN: The open road

BIRTHDAY: January 10

STANCE: Goofy

FAVORITE TYPE OF RIDING: I love all skateboarding, but my favorite is pools and cement skateparks.

Q&A with Heidi Fitzgerald

How old were you when you started?
I got my first real wooden skateboard when I was 14, while visiting my dad for the summer in Virginia. My stepbrother was getting a shop board, and I wanted one.

What got you into the sport?
Growing up, I was a military brat. We moved a bunch, and I got to see these plastic skateboards sometime in the late 1970s cruising around the boardwalk in Florida. I think from that point forth, I saw something in skateboarding, but not until I moved to Texas did I fall in love with it. Once I talked my mom into dropping me off at the skatepark, I was hooked.

What were you doing before you started skateboarding?
I played a lot of soccer and after school I hung out with my friends. I loved to be outside and doing something active always kept me busy.

Any advice for beginners?
First off, support your local mom-and-pop skate shop and buy a real skateboard. Make sure you have the proper equipment before you start. While learning, wear protective gear. Take lessons if you need them or watch a trick-tip video—they can really help. But most of all, have fun.

What type of music do you listen to?
I listen to every kind of music out there. Music is a release, and I don't limit myself to one genre. When I'm skating, I tend to listen to punk rock or heavy metal. It gets me going.

Favorite groups?
Bad Brains, Operation Ivy, D.R.I., Bad Religion, Minor Threat

Signature move/favorite trick?
I love to do ollies, frontside mostly, but backside is fun too—the feeling of floating in the air with nothing under you except your board. I love that you can do ollies anywhere—on ramps and streets and in pools.

How did you get to be you?
I had a lot of help from my parents and friends. With their support and guidance, I grew to be a very determined and passionate person. I learned to always better myself and to never be afraid to try anything. Always keep your drive alive.

What can a kid do to be like you?
Be the best person you can be and treat everyone the way you'd like to be treated. Most of all, have fun and let everyone see you smile.

What do you like to do outside of skateboarding?
Outside of skateboarding, I like to travel, play with our cat, write, play video games, and read when I can, such as the Harry Potter series and any John Grisham book.

Frontside Pool Grind

Pool coping is usually made of marble or concrete. Doing grinds on pool coping feels very different from grinding steel or plastic coping; usually it is much rougher and bigger. And sometimes when your trucks grind the coping, it sparks! If you are new to skateboarding in pools, first concentrate on comfortably building up speed and learning how to carve the walls. Slowly work your way up to mastering grinds.

1. Drop into the pool from the shallow end and carve the walls for a few turns to help build up your speed.
2. As you skate up to the top edge of the pool, your chest should face the coping you're about to grind. Again, this is what makes it a frontside grind. (Having your back to the spot you're about to grind is called a backside grind.)
3. Compress your knees as your body travels up the transition of the pool.
4. Use your arms and upper body to steer your weight.
5. As you approach the pool coping, allow the rear wheel on the toeside of your skateboard to roll up and lap over the coping. This will cause your rear axle to begin grinding the coping.
6. Keep your weight on the rear leg while using the front leg to steer your body through the trick.
7. Turn 180 degrees and bring your body back down into the pool's transition. Remember: Bend your knees and keep your speed up!

How Skateboarding got Started

No one really knows the exact date that skateboards came into being but we do know kids tore apart their roller skates and nailed the wheels to planks of wood.

In 1959, the first commercial skateboard, the Roller Derby Skateboard, was made. As surfing grew in popularity so did skateboarding. Skateboarding was known as "sidewalk surfing" because riders rode both waves and cement in the same style.

1960s: Skateboarding briefly went mainstream in the mid-1960s with several surfboard companies manufacturing skateboards and sponsoring teams. National television networks broadcasted international competitions and major advertisers began sponsoring these events. Innovations of all kinds were crucial to the 1960s skateboarding revolution, including better deck construction and safety gear. These changes improved the quality of skateboards and brought about a broad expansion of tricks and riding styles. However, as soon as it boomed, by 1966 skateboarding had almost disappeared completely.

1970s: The next skateboarding boom began in 1973 with the introduction of urethane wheels, a pioneering innovation that provided skateboarders with greater traction, speed, and overall performance. Precision wheel bearings and lighter, skateboard-specific pivoting trucks followed. In 1977 Alan Gelfand invented the no-handed "ollie" air, a move that would completely change the course of skateboarding. But again, at the end of the '70s skateboarding went into another slump. Insurance costs and safety concerns closed the doors of most skateparks. Soon, skateboarders began adapting their tricks to backyard pools, ditches, and full-pipes.

1980s: In the early '80s skateboarders quickly developed additional ollie variations, which led to a fast-paced progression of airs and more technical, difficult tricks. The late '80s saw the close of most remaining parks. Since most skateboarders couldn't afford expensive vert ramps, many began returning to backyard pools and/or adapting freestyle flat-ground tricks to street skating.

1990s: Throughout the '90s vert skating dropped in popularity as most skateboarders came to favor skating wooden "mini" ramps or exploring the freedom of the streets; skating ledges, handrails, curbs, and stairs. This era also saw the rise of skater-owned companies, wherein current athletes and retired pros alike began creating brands, building teams of riders, starting magazines, and filming videos.

Today, the most popular form of skateboarding remains street skating. Vert skating is making a comeback, however, due to the popularity of competitions like the X Games and to the large number of municipal skateparks being built in towns throughout the United States. These new parks are helping to create strong skateboarding communities all over the country. Skateboarding is in every media source, and its influence can be felt in everything including fashion, music, film, television, publishing, and advertising.

etnies

Jimmy Marcus

HOMETOWN: Clearwater, Florida
BIRTHDAY: May 19
STANCE: Goofy
FAVORITE TYPE OF RIDING: Anything made of concrete

Q&A with Jimmy Marcus

How old were you when you started?
6 or 7

What were you doing at the age of 10?
Just skating and having fun with friends, laughing, and having a good time. At an early age, don't worry about going pro—that will come in time.

What got you into the sport?
My grandma, mom, and dad got me a plastic Roller Derby skateboard for Christmas when I was 5. The older kids were already skating in the neighborhood, and I saw how fun it was. Then I got another board just as good as theirs. I never turned back—it was on.

Any advice for beginners?
Go out, have fun, and don't listen to what anybody else says because it's all about having fun and creating your own style.

What type of music do you listen to?
Reggae in the morning, punk rock in the afternoon, and Bob Dylan in the evening

Favorite groups?
MC5, Lynyrd Skynyrd, Dead Kennedys, Cro-Mags, Led Zeppelin, GG Allin

Highlights of your career?
Receiving my first pro-model skateboard on Scum Skates, meeting all my childhood heroes, and last but not least, meeting the love of my life

Signature move/favorite trick?
Frontside invert to fakie and Smith grinds, because they are difficult and fun, and you can lock a Smith grind and grind forever

How did you get to be you?
Hard work, skating every day, and progressing to where I'm stoked on my skating

How does a kid get to be as good as you?
Skate every day, have fun, and learn tricks as they come. Watch videos by yourself and with friends.

What do you like to do outside of skateboarding?
Surf, play golf, fish, barbecue, and watch NASCAR

Frontside Ollie Tail Grab in Pool

To do this trick correctly, you'll want to know how to do a huge ollie in a pool. This is one of the oldest, coolest tricks in pool skating, but it is also a bit difficult to learn. Be patient. This trick is worth the extra effort!

1. First, carve the walls of the pool for a few turns to help build up your speed.
2. Your chest should be facing the wall as you skate up the transition toward the coping. Again, this is what makes it a frontside trick.
3. Bend your knees and use your arms and upper body to steer your weight as you travel up the transition.
4. As you approach the pool coping, pop an ollie with as much power and snap as you can. This will propel your body and board into the air, above the lip of the pool.
5. As you're traveling through the air, use your back hand to grab the tail of your skateboard. (This is where the name "ollie tail grab" comes from.)
6. Keep the rear leg tucked up toward your body while boning out the front leg to stylishly steer your body through the trick.
7. Turn 180 degrees and bring your body back down into the pool's transition.
8. Remember: Bend your knees as you land and keep your speed up for that fast-approaching next wall!

Skateboard Lingo

air: To feel weightless. When you and your skateboard are still connected and no longer have contact with the ground, and you feel kind of elated—you're getting air.

backside: When you're turning or doing your trick, you can still see your feet and where your board is going. This is the easiest basic position for most skaters, but some people feel more comfortable going frontside. If your back is first approaching the terrain you're about to skate on, then you are doing the trick backside.

boardslide: Sliding the underside of your board sideways along a curb, ledge, handrail, pool, or piece of wood.

compression/to compress: Bending your knees and torso flattens out the base of your skateboard and makes your body more compact as you're traveling up a transition. This helps you to gain speed and prepare for springing onto or off a jump, ledge, rail, etc.

coping: Usually made of steel, plastic, marble, or concrete; it is the material placed at the edge or lip of most skateboard ramps, backyard pools, and concrete skateparks (and occasionally on skateboard structures and transitioned obstacles).

drop in: Dropping in is when you lean forward and drop into the transition or surface. When you first learn how to drop into a ramp or pool, you must exaggerate your lean or you will probably eat it. Pretend you are touching the nose of your board as you drop in to help you lean forward.

fakie: When the skateboarder's feet are positioned for going one way, but he or she ends up riding the other way, this is called fakie. Normally, the back foot is on the tail, but when riding fakie it will often be on the nose of the board. Basically, skating backward.

frontside: Blind-sided turn with your body facing the ramp. As you're approaching a vert wall/handrail/tabletop jump/pool transition and your chest is facing the terrain you're about to skate, then you are doing the trick frontside.

goofy foot: Standing with your right foot placed at the front end of the board.

hand plant: When you are upside down with one hand on the coping, while compressing the board to your body with your other hand before bringing the board back onto the surface you're riding.

ollie: Alan "Ollie" Gelfand invented the ollie in 1976. To ollie you snap the tail of the board down while sliding your front foot up along the skateboard and jumping. Just like backside and frontside airs, the ollie is the backbone of most skateboarding tricks. Learn to master the ollie before moving on to more difficult tricks.

regular foot: Standing with your left foot placed at the front end of the board.

switchstance: Changing skating positions to the opposite of what comes naturally. Some pro skaters are able to do this easily and find switchstance just as comfortable as skating their usual way. They're really good.

tail slide: Putting pressure on the tail of your board causing it to slide at the same time. Tailslides can be fun on painted or waxed curbs, vert ramps, and in pools.

transition: This refers to the curvature of any surfaces you might be riding. Some transitions are quick (like a bank-to-wallride), and some are gradual (like the transition of a large vert ramp).

vert: Vert is an abbreviation of the word "vertical," and it means a ramp or jump wherein the transition curves upward to a 90-degree angle. Transitions that go to vert are designed to shoot the rider straight up into the air and back down into the transition.

Many of these skate definitions apply to snowboarding too.

On the Edge SNOWBOARDING

Patty Segovia

Designed by
Matthew Eberhart, Evil Eye Design, Inc.

Contributing consultant
Arlie John Carstens

Meredith® Books

First Edition
ISBN 978-0-696-23540-5
We welcome your comments and suggestions.
Write to us at: Meredith Books,
1716 Locust St., Des Moines, IA 50309-3023
Visit us at meredithbooks.com

Photo Credits:
(c) Patty Segovia, pages 4 (top left, bottom right), 9 (bottom), 10, 11, 12, 13 (top left), 17 (top right, bottom left), 18, 19, 22, 23; (c) Christian Brecheis, page 14; (c) Jesse Brown, pages 3, 8 (top right), 9 (top), 21 (middle); (c) Christy Chaloux/Runway Films, pages 14-15; (c) Neil DaCosta, page 7; (c) Stan Evans, page 6; (c) Matt Lancaster, page 5 (top); (c) Embry Rucker, page 11; (c) Chris Wellhausen, page 19; (c) TMB Photo, pages 2, 4 (top left), 5 (middle), 12, 24 (top right); (c) Big Bear Mountain Resorts, pages 8 (top left, bottom), 16 (middle, bottom right), 21 (top left); (c) Matthew Eberhart, pages 16 (top left), 21 (top right); Shutterstock.com: (c) Eric Limon, cover, pages 1 (top), 13 (right), 24 (bottom); (c) Galina Barskaya, pages 1, 5 (bottom); (c) Eugen Shevchenko, page 4; (c) Jose Manuel Gelpi Diaz, page 5 (bottom); (c) Kaleb Timberlake, page 12 (middle); (c) Comhnall Dods, page 12 (bottom right); (c) @erics, page 13 (silhouette); (c) Action Photos, page 16 (top right); (c) Brian Finestone, page 16 (bottom left); (c) WizData, Inc., pages 17 (top left), 21 (bottom); (c) Maxim Petrichuk, page 20 (left); (c) Mikael Damkier, page 20 (top right); (c) Dvoretskiy Igor Vladimirovich, page 20 (middle)

Rob Kingwell

HOMETOWN: Jackson Hole, Wyoming
BIRTHDAY: June 25
FAVORITE TYPE OF RIDING: Freeriding
STANCE: Regular, 18, −9, 22 inches centered

Favorite groups?
Snow Patrol, Pearl Jam, Bush, Talib Kweli, Jay Z, and Biomecca

Signature move/favorite snowboarding trick?
I invented a trick called a Satoflip or Kingerflip, which is like doing a frontside McTwist in a halfpipe. There are only a couple of people in the world who can do it like me. One of the Japanese riders did it absolutely, ridiculously huge at the Olympics and I was so honored and excited because that trick moved beyond just me doing it. It is a really cool feeling to create something new in the sport you love.

How does a kid get to be as good as you?
If you want to get good, you have to ride, ride, and ride some more. If you want to get good you have to get out and go after it. Get your parents to move you to a place where you can ride every weekend, if not every day. Watch videos, jump on the trampoline, skate, go to the gym and get strong. You need passion for what you want to do and go the extra mile to get better. Don't worry about getting sponsored so much; if you are good enough they will come to you. Just focus on getting a little bit better, each and every day.

Highlights of your career?
U.S. Open Halfpipe Champion; X Games: bronze medal in slopestyle; Gravity Games: silver medal in quarterpipe; World Championships: bronze medal in halfpipe; and Mt. Baker Legendary Banked Slalom: bronze medal.

Q&A with Rob Kingwell

How old were you when you started?
12

What got you into the sport?
One of my best friends had tried it a couple of times before and talked me into going out and pointing it down an ice-covered road behind my house. I was hooked then and there.

Any advice for beginners?
The first couple days you can get pretty beat up. I remember we put pillows in our snow pants and duct-taped plastic bags to our butts when we were first learning. They have better waterproofing on the pants now and actually have butt pads you can wear to minimize the pain. I would also recommend taking a lesson from a snowboard instructor. They will get you riding in no time and you will be ripping around with your friends much faster than if you just go it on your own.

When I was a kid I was really into BMX, skateboarding, and drawing. I was just a regular kid in a mountain town, and I never dreamed that snowboarding could actually become a career. I just went out and had fun with my friends and enjoyed being a kid.

Frontside Stalefish on Quarterpipe

Try this on a quarterpipe with a long runway, lots of transition (curve), and at least a foot of vert at the top of the wall. A well-made quarterpipe will give you enough airtime to really throw this trick high in the air.

1. Approach the lip of the jump with your knees compressed and the base of your board riding flat against the snow.
2. As you hit the lip and spring into the air, make sure you have enough speed to toss your legs and the board underneath your feet far out in front of you.
3. Once in the air you must grab the heelside edge of your board with your back hand around your back leg. It takes a lot of effort to reach back there, but it's worth it!
4. As you come back in for your landing you'll want to let go of the board, suck up your knees, and land flat on the base of your board.
5. Ride away smoothly. You've just done one of the coolest tricks in snowboarding.

General Tips

know how to fall: Knowing how to fall properly can reduce your chance of injury. Learn to fall by practicing on the grass or on a soft surface. When you begin to lose your balance, crouch down, reducing the distance of the fall. If you find yourself falling, tuck, roll, and try not to catch yourself with your hands or arms. Teach yourself to not put your hands in front of you during a fall—this could lead to a break or bad muscle sprain. If at all possible, relax your body when falling rather than falling stiff.

fast friends: Bring a buddy whenever you go snowboarding, especially in the backcountry or when riding unfamiliar terrain. It's good to have a friend around in case anything goes wrong.

stretch: Don't forget to stretch and warm up before you snowboard; you don't want to pull any muscles.

water: Snowboarding is a vigorous athletic activity; always remember to drink plenty of water before, during, and after snowboarding. Dehydration can cause muscle cramps, nausea, and a feeling of lightheadedness.

Erin Comstock

HOMETOWN: Salt Lake City, Utah

BIRTHDAY: January 2

FAVORITE TYPE OF RIDING: I love the powder and the park. I think whenever I am with my friends, that is my favorite riding.

STANCE: 22 inches wide with 21 degrees on my front foot and 21 degrees on my back foot.

Q&A with Erin Comstock

How old were you when you started?
I started skiing when I was 2. When I was 12, I wanted to try snowboarding. After going a couple of times, I saved up money to buy my first snowboard at age 14, which was a Burton Air. From there I just followed my passion. Thankfully, my mom insisted my grades stay up if I wanted to keep riding.

Signature move/favorite trick?
I guess I am known for my frontside boardslides, but my favorite trick is frontside spin off a jump.

What got you into the sport?
I love skiing, and all of my guy friends started to snowboard, so I joined them.

Any advice for beginners?
Yes! Don't get frustrated, and make sure you are using products that are up to date! That's very important!

What type of music do you listen to?
I like all kinds of music, except for country and crazy-hard metal.

Favorite groups?
Lately I have been listening to the Justin Timberlake CD. I also really like Fischerspooner, and Euro music is awesome to listen to.

Highlights of your career?
Cover of *Transworld*, X Games, and traveling the world

How does a kid get to be as good as you?
Well, I always like to say that your mind is your biggest power. If you have the confidence and the passion to do something, I feel anything is possible.

What can a kid do to be like you?
I love exercising and eating healthy. I feel this has kept my body running properly. I also like to take glucosamine to help my joints. I am super-dedicated to snowboarding. I feel that having this kind of passion helps me be who I am.

What do you like to do outside of snowboarding?
I also love soccer. I played two years of college soccer in San Jose. I enjoy surfing, wake surfing, volleyball, and cooking. I like to be active all the time.

Tree Jibbing

OK, this trick can be tricky. Basically, you're hopping onto a fallen tree and sliding down it. This is very fun! Sometimes the log will be on the ground (easiest) and sometimes it might be partially stuck in the ground and lying at an angle (more difficult), or bowed like a rainbow (experts only).

1. Dull the edges of your board before trying this one; you don't want sharp edges digging into the tree.
2. Make sure there is wax on the base of your board so you can slide quickly and in control.
3. Make sure there is enough space between the run-up to the log and the landing area.
4. Try to have just enough speed to ollie up onto the log, but don't carry too much speed.
5. Keep your arms outstretched and your weight evenly centered across the log as you slide it.
6. You'll want to stay light on your feet the whole way through the trick so that you can pop back onto the snow with style and grace.

Equipment

Snowboarding, unlike skateboarding, takes a lot of time to get ready to do. Also, a lot of equipment is involved: boots, bindings, snowboards, helmet, and safety straps.

alpine: This type of snowboard is skinny and hard. They are usually longer than freestyle boards. There is a side cut to help with carving. The majority of them are flat in the back like downhill skis.

bindings: The bindings are a piece of equipment that attaches your boot to the snowboard. When using hard boots the bindings look like metal plates (clicker bindings). You attach them by stepping onto them with your hard boots and presto they clamp onto your boots. Make sure that you originally put your bindings at the right spot so that you will be comfortable.

boots: In snowboarding there are two different kinds of boots: soft boots and hard boots. Snowboarders wear soft boots. Soft boots are very light but still help you get the support that you need. They are flexible for doing tricks. Soft boots have two parts: an inner liner that gives you support (bladder), and an outer boot that has a sole with treads for traction.

freestyle/freeriding: These boards are the most common in snowboarding. They are usually less stiff and shorter in length. They have "twin tips" (nose and tail are shaped identical). This allows you to ride down either backward or forward.

helmet: Snowboarders wear helmets, especially the smarter ones. Helmets help prevent you from getting a concussion. You should make sure you invest in a quality helmet. Some helmets now contain gel pads in them to give extra protection.

safety strap: Because of liability concerns, ski resorts require that you wear a safety strap while riding on the chairlift. They don't want a snowboard falling off your foot and potentially landing on someone's head. This strap connects your front leg to the front of your binding. If your front binding breaks, the strap will be connected to the board.

snowboards: Each one is designed for different types of riding: alpine and freestyle (freeriding). Alpine boards are known as racing boards, whereas freestyle boards are used in the half-pipe and snowparks for doing tricks and catching big air!

Todd Richards

HOMETOWN: Encinitas, California

BIRTHDAY: December 28

FAVORITE TYPE OF RIDING: I really like to ride soft snow—powder is always fun, but a day with 6 inches of powder in the park can be just as fun as a huge dump.

STANCE: 22.5 inches, ducked a little. I never really measure the angles—just go with what feels good.

Q&A with Todd Richards

How old were you when you started?
I was 15 when I first tried snowboarding. I didn't really get into snowboarding for a few more years, after I went away to school in New Hampshire.

Signature move/favorite trick?
Well, I did come up with a few over the years. The wet cat is a backside 900 that combines a flat 360 with a McTwist and a frontside inverted 900, basically the same thing, just frontside.

What got you into the sport?
My love for skateboarding and the crappy winters the East Coast handed us

Any advice for beginners?
Don't get frustrated; patience is your friend. You will get it; some just take more time than others.

What type of music do you listen to?
Mostly faster alternative rock; not that crap you hear on the radio, though

Favorite groups?
Pinback; At the Drive-In; Wolf Parade; Goodbye, Blue Monday; Years Around the Sun

How does a kid get to be as good as you?
Don't concentrate on how good you are; concentrate on the process of getting there.

What do you like to do outside of snowboarding?
Surfing is my biggest love right now. Hang out with my family and go skating and surfing with my kids

Corked Indy Backside 540 in Halfpipe

This trick can be performed a few different ways—a flat spin (base of the board horizontal with the ground), corked (semi-inverted spin), or an inverted spin (spinning while upside-down). Here, Todd is doing a corked 540. Notice how he's sideways but not fully upside-down? Radical! Before trying this trick in the halfpipe, learn backside 180s and 360s on natural hits and terrain park jumps. Once you have backside 360s solid, all you have to do is add another 180.

1. This trick requires a lot of momentum; drop into the halfpipe with enough speed and wind-up to rotate the full 540-degree spin.
2. Approach the backside wall riding forward; keep your weight on your heels. Square up your front shoulder and switch your weight to your toe side edge just as you near the lip of the transition. Compress your knees!
3. As you spring off the lip, drop your back shoulder and turn your head in the direction you're going to spin. Remember: The head leads the body.
4. As you rotate, try to have an idea of where you'd like to land further down the halfpipe. This will keep you from shooting out onto the deck or tossing yourself to the flat bottom.
5. Once airborne, at the 270-degree mark of the rotation (that's one-and-a-half spins), suck your knees up to your chest and grab the toe side edge of the board with your back hand. Grab between the bindings, this is what makes it an Indy grab.
6. With 90 degrees left to rotate, set up for the landing. Keep your legs bent and ready to absorb the impact. Stay centered over the board.
7. Land with your base flat so that you ride away smooth and with enough speed to hit the next wall.

JOYRIDE

What is a snowboard made of?

core: The core of the board is what's found between all the exterior materials. It is composed of wood, composite material, or foam.

fiberglass: Fiberglass is placed on top of the core. This gives a board extra strength. Many boards have two layers of fiberglass to increase the durability and strength of the board.

steel edges: Every board has a steel edge border. This border is what gives you the power grip to carve and turn.

top sheet: A plastic coating on the fiberglass protects your board from impact.

base: The base is the bottom of the snowboard. It is made of polyethylene or P-Tex. There are three types of bases: extended, sintered, or graphite.

extended base: This is the least expensive base, the easiest to repair, and the one that lasts the longest. However, it is slower and doesn't absorb wax very well.

sintered base: This is more durable, but harder to fix. You get what you pay for—the speed and wax absorption are awesome.

graphite base: When it comes to speed, this is the ultimate base. Racers always use graphite-based boards.

Silvia Mittermüller

HOMETOWN: Munich, Germany

BIRTHDAY: August 8

FAVORITE TYPE OF RIDING: A fresh-shaped park after it gets fresh snow. Yes, I know some people will hate me for not saying powder.

STANCE: Goofy, 22 inches, +12 degrees; −12 degrees

Q&A with Silvia Mittermüller

How old were you when you started?
14

Signature move/favorite trick?
I love anything that feels safe, smooth, clean, and 100 percent under control. Long grabs and clean landings can make any trick a favorite of the moment: quality over quantity.

What got you into the sport?
This may sound crazy, but my parents wanted to learn how to snowboard first. Then I thought if my parents can learn how to snowboard, I can too. So we learned together, the entire family. We have been riding together for nine years.

What were you doing before you started snowboarding?
I was going to school. In my free time, I tried many different kinds of sports with my friends and family. Sports have always made me happy. But also school is really important. As much as you love a sport, you should never quit school for it. I finished school even though I was already on the national team at that point and traveling everywhere to do the pipe World Cup. So don't drop out of school.

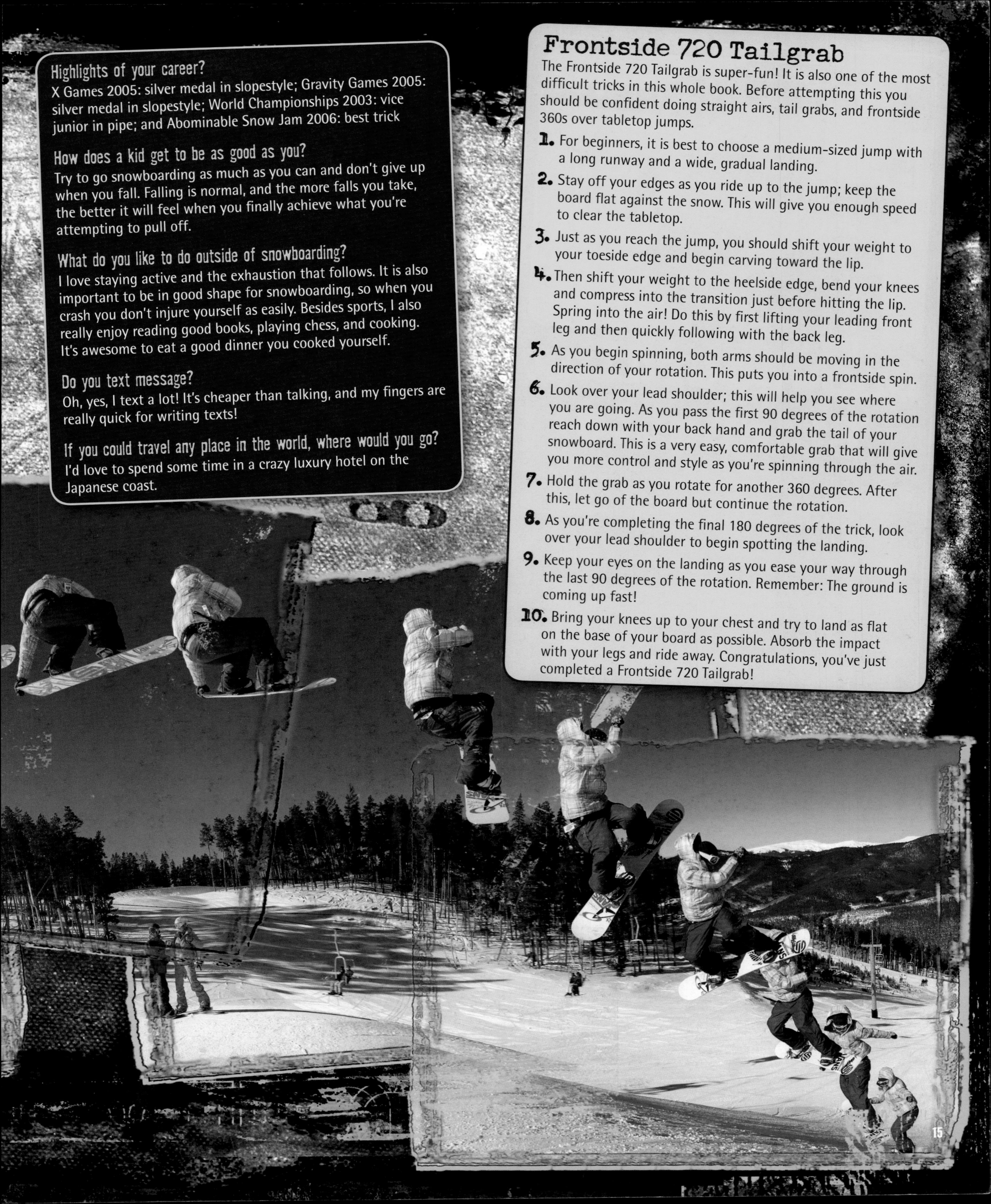

Highlights of your career?
X Games 2005: silver medal in slopestyle; Gravity Games 2005: silver medal in slopestyle; World Championships 2003: vice junior in pipe; and Abominable Snow Jam 2006: best trick

How does a kid get to be as good as you?
Try to go snowboarding as much as you can and don't give up when you fall. Falling is normal, and the more falls you take, the better it will feel when you finally achieve what you're attempting to pull off.

What do you like to do outside of snowboarding?
I love staying active and the exhaustion that follows. It is also important to be in good shape for snowboarding, so when you crash you don't injure yourself as easily. Besides sports, I also really enjoy reading good books, playing chess, and cooking. It's awesome to eat a good dinner you cooked yourself.

Do you text message?
Oh, yes, I text a lot! It's cheaper than talking, and my fingers are really quick for writing texts!

If you could travel any place in the world, where would you go?
I'd love to spend some time in a crazy luxury hotel on the Japanese coast.

Frontside 720 Tailgrab

The Frontside 720 Tailgrab is super-fun! It is also one of the most difficult tricks in this whole book. Before attempting this you should be confident doing straight airs, tail grabs, and frontside 360s over tabletop jumps.

1. For beginners, it is best to choose a medium-sized jump with a long runway and a wide, gradual landing.
2. Stay off your edges as you ride up to the jump; keep the board flat against the snow. This will give you enough speed to clear the tabletop.
3. Just as you reach the jump, you should shift your weight to your toeside edge and begin carving toward the lip.
4. Then shift your weight to the heelside edge, bend your knees and compress into the transition just before hitting the lip. Spring into the air! Do this by first lifting your leading front leg and then quickly following with the back leg.
5. As you begin spinning, both arms should be moving in the direction of your rotation. This puts you into a frontside spin.
6. Look over your lead shoulder; this will help you see where you are going. As you pass the first 90 degrees of the rotation reach down with your back hand and grab the tail of your snowboard. This is a very easy, comfortable grab that will give you more control and style as you're spinning through the air.
7. Hold the grab as you rotate for another 360 degrees. After this, let go of the board but continue the rotation.
8. As you're completing the final 180 degrees of the trick, look over your lead shoulder to begin spotting the landing.
9. Keep your eyes on the landing as you ease your way through the last 90 degrees of the rotation. Remember: The ground is coming up fast!
10. Bring your knees up to your chest and try to land as flat on the base of your board as possible. Absorb the impact with your legs and ride away. Congratulations, you've just completed a Frontside 720 Tailgrab!

Snowboarding Etiquette

- Always keep your snowboard under control so you are able to stop at any moment. At the start of your run, give way to other riders and check your backside and frontside before starting down the mountain.
- Know your limits; remember lessons are always available.
- If you are in a busy area, it is your responsibility to avoid collisions, be aware of your surroundings and other riders.
- Never stop or sit down in the middle of a run and make sure you are visible to other riders.
- Be aware of the rules of the snow resort and follow all trail signs.
- Look at the landing area before attempting a jump. It is wise to have a friend be a spotter when hitting a jump.
- Due to tree branches, bends or variable snow conditions (rain, snow, fog) sometimes your vision is not as clear, proceed with caution.
- Always snowboard with a friend and never snowboard alone. Accidents can happen.

Vans

Lucas Magoon

HOMETOWN: Rutland, Vermont
BIRTHDAY: February 10
FAVORITE TYPE OF RIDING: Park and powder
STANCE: Goofy

Q&A with Lucas Magoon

How old were you when you started?
4

What were you doing at the age of 10?
Same things I'm doing now

Signature move/favorite trick?
Nollying into tricks, bagelin' out because it's fun.

What got you into the sport?
I was a skier until I walked into a snowboard shop that was next to the ski shop where my mom worked. Once I saw a snowboard video, I was hooked. My mom got me my first snowboard. We would drive up to a little mountain called Pico. I would go down and up all day long until the bunny hill was too slow for me. Then I would go booming double blacks all day.

Any advice for beginners?
Just that you must love to snowboard. Loving going up on the coldest, snowiest days and not wanting to leave—that's what loving snowboarding is all about.

What type of music do you listen to?
Hip-hop

Favorite groups?
Dipset All-Stars

Highlights of your career?
Winning $10,000 and meeting the love of my life

How does a kid get to be as good as you?
Love snowboarding and push yourself to the limit.

How did you get to be you?
Growing up meeting the people I met and being around the things I was around. Love makes me who I am.

Do you text message?
Who doesn't text these days?

What do you like to do outside of snowboarding?
Everyday kid stuff: being with friends and of course being with the one girl whom I'll never stop loving.

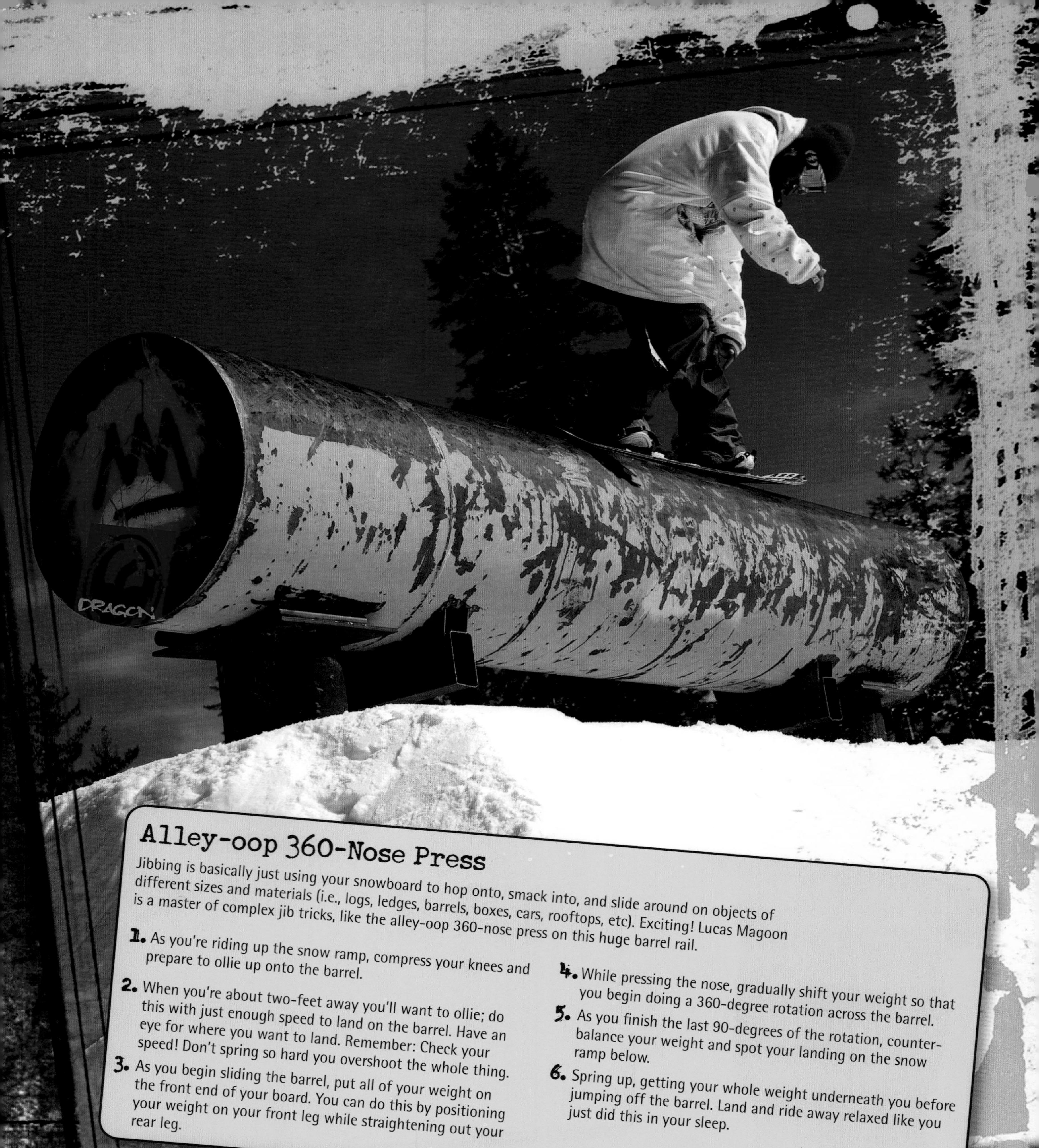

Alley-oop 360-Nose Press

Jibbing is basically just using your snowboard to hop onto, smack into, and slide around on objects of different sizes and materials (i.e., logs, ledges, barrels, boxes, cars, rooftops, etc). Exciting! Lucas Magoon is a master of complex jib tricks, like the alley-oop 360-nose press on this huge barrel rail.

1. As you're riding up the snow ramp, compress your knees and prepare to ollie up onto the barrel.
2. When you're about two-feet away you'll want to ollie; do this with just enough speed to land on the barrel. Have an eye for where you want to land. Remember: Check your speed! Don't spring so hard you overshoot the whole thing.
3. As you begin sliding the barrel, put all of your weight on the front end of your board. You can do this by positioning your weight on your front leg while straightening out your rear leg.
4. While pressing the nose, gradually shift your weight so that you begin doing a 360-degree rotation across the barrel.
5. As you finish the last 90-degrees of the rotation, counter-balance your weight and spot your landing on the snow ramp below.
6. Spring up, getting your whole weight underneath you before jumping off the barrel. Land and ride away relaxed like you just did this in your sleep.

How Snowboarding got Started

Snowboarding, a combination of surfing and skateboarding on snow, was invented about 35 years ago.

In 1963, a skateboarder named Tom Sims made a "ski board" out of plywood. He was only in eighth grade and he did this in his shop class. He later formed a company called Sims Snowboards. Another credited snowboard inventor was Sherman Poppen. In 1965, Poppen designed a snowboard called a Snurfer. He bolted two skis together and attached a rope to the nose of the board to help with balance and steering. In 1969, Dimitrije Milovich was goofing around sliding down snowy hills on cafeteria trays when he got the idea to make a snowboard with metal edges. He was attending college in upstate New York when he came up with this idea.

1970s: In 1972, Milovich launched his new snowboard company, Winterstick. In 1979, Jake Burton Carpenter started making snowboards out of fiberglass in Vermont. Soon after, he added strap-in bindings to help riders feel more secure on the board. This also made controlling the board easier. During this era, the snowboarding community was very small; most everyone knew each other, and riders shared knowledge in hopes of progressing the sport.

1980s: In the mid-1980s, all snowboard manufacturers began building steel edges into the sides of snowboards and using P-Tex bases, giving riders greater control on ice and hard pack snow. High backs were added to bindings. This important innovation made linking backside and frontside turns more fun, and provided riders more control at faster speeds. After nearly 20 years, the snowboarding craze had finally arrived! Still, many ski resorts would not let snowboarders use their slopes due to its perceived rebel nature. Indeed, by 1985 only 39 of 600 ski areas in the U.S. allowed snowboards. In the late-1980s, freestyle snowboarders like Terry Kidwell, Shaun Palmer, and Craig Kelly began earnestly adapting skateboarding tricks to snowboarding terrain, in the process steering the sports toward the halfpipes, and terrain parks to come.

1990s: In 1990 Vail became the first major ski resort to offer an in-bounds obstacle area called a snowboard park. The popularity of snowboarding videos featuring progressive freestyle tricks and big mountain riding exploded in the 1990s. In 1998, snowboarding made its Olympic debut in Nagano, Japan. The recognition helped snowboarders gain acceptance within the mainstream sports world.

2000s: At the 2002 Winter Olympics in Salt Lake City, Utah, the competition halfpipe was 525-feet long with transitions 17-feet deep. This was the first competition 'Superpipe' the world had ever seen, and it allowed the athletes to do bigger airs than ever before. Americans Shawn White and Danny Kass won the 2006 Olympics in Torino, Italy. These exciting Olympic events, as well as other televised competitions, have helped to make snowboarding a popular sport, one of the fastest growing in the country.

Leanne Pelosi

HOMETOWN: Calgary, Alberta, Canada

BIRTHDAY: December 9

FAVORITE TYPE OF RIDING: I like riding everything, but I find myself in the park more often than not.

STANCE: Goofy

Q&A with Leanne Pelosi

How old were you when you started?
16

Signature move/favorite trick?
I'm known for spinning into rails. I can do 270s a variety of ways, but I also spin cab and frontside 720s. I am working on backside and switch backside this year. My favorite spin is anything I can poke with style.

What were you doing before you started snowboarding?
I used to play soccer and field hockey. I also liked to play outside, playing games like hide-and-seek with my friends and using a Ouija board. On a sunny day, I would get my dad to turn the sprinklers on, and we would put out a big slippery banana. We had fun sliding on that.

Any advice for beginners?
Wear wrist guards, a helmet, and a butt pad for the first few days. Once you get the hang of turning and edge control, you won't have a sore butt anymore.

What got you into the sport?
I thought it looked really cool. My friends were snowboarding, and I was skiing. I eventually convinced my parents to buy me a snowboard for Christmas. My brother and I shared it. I would buy snowboard magazines before I even started snowboarding. Later when I saw my friends with their snowboards, I wanted to do the same thing.

What type of music do you listen to?
I listen to everything. It depends on what mood I'm in. I like the new electro-pop that is out and I also like 1980s music, punk, country, and more.

Favorite groups?
TV on the Radio, Trevor Andrew, Tilly and the Wall, Madonna, The Organ, Tegan and Sarah, Jem, AFI, The Ramones, Social Distortion

Highlights of your career?
Winning the U.S. Open Rail Jam twice and also winning a car at the contest. I also won *Transworld* Rider of the Year, Reader's Choice, and *Snowboarder* magazine's Rider of the Year in 2005.

How does a kid get to be as good as you?
You need to snowboard every day possible and try new tricks with your friends.

What do you like to do outside of snowboarding?
I like to take photos, play with my video camera, run, bike, go to the gym, read books and magazines, run a snowboard camp, and assist in designing the equipment I use.

Boardslide on Handrail

Before taking the trick to a down rail like this one, you should first know how to ollie on flat ground and boardslide flat rails and boxes. Once you've learned those basic skills, you can move on to sliding handrails with confidence.

1. Before attempting this trick, remember to dull your edges!
2. Approach the rail with enough speed to ollie up onto it. The faster you go, the less you will have to ollie. As you do this, look down the center of the rail.
3. As soon as you're on the rail, remember to bend your knees and distribute your weight evenly over the rail.
4. Control your balance with your shoulders and arms; this will make you more stable as you're sliding down the rail.
5. As you approach the end of the rail, ollie off it lightly, and be ready to compress your knees.
6. Stomp the landing.

Snowboarding Lingo

avalanche transceiver: This is an electronic beacon worn by backcountry and big mountain snowboarders. It is used to help a search party quickly locate a rider buried in an avalanche. In the event a rider becomes buried, everyone in the party turns their beacons to "receive" mode, which allows them to hear the signal of the buried rider. As the search party moves closer, the signal gets stronger. Once located, probes and shovels are used to dig the rider out of the avalanche as quickly as possible.

backside: A backside turn is when a snowboarder turns his/her back into the turn first.

base: The underside of a snowboard is constructed out of a porous plastic material called P-Tex. Applying wax to the base both protects the P-Tex layer and increases speed and control on the hill.

bindings: The gear used to hold a rider's feet onto the snowboard.

catch an edge: When the steel edge of the board digs into the snow.

directional shape: A snowboard shape and construction technique common in resort and big mountain freeriding boards. Designed generally to be ridden in one direction, the tail is usually stiffer than the nose and stance is set back of center.

edge: A band of steel that runs along either side of a snowboard; its function is to help the rider carve on hard-pack snow and ice.

freeriding: A style of snowboarding focusing on all mountain terrain; cruising, natural hits, trees, cliff drops, and powder.

freestyle: A style of snowboarding that emphasizes park and pipe riding. Freestyle snowboarders generally use shorter boards, soft boots, and more flexible bindings.

frontside turn: When a rider goes into the turn chest first.

halfpipe: A halfpipe is a U-shaped trench wherein snowboarders carve the walls and perform aerial maneuvers. The sides are usually about 17-to-22 feet high. It can be as long as 400 feet and as wide as 50 feet.

heelside (aka backside) edge: The edge of the side of the snowboard closest to the heels of your boot.

sideslip: Sliding sideways down a hill with your snowboard, often done to slow one's speed.

skating: When the front foot is strapped to the snowboard and one pushing with the other foot and sliding. This technique is used when traveling across flat ground or traversing slight inclines.

switchstance: Riding opposite of how you would normally ride.

toeside (aka frontside) edge: The edge of the side of the snowboard closest to the toes of your boot.

twin tip: A snowboard shape and construction technique —common in freestyle riding—where the nose and tail are identical and the stance is centered or slightly back of center.